Motherland, Stories and Poems from Louisiana

Motherland,
Stories and Poems from Louisiana

Lynn Hoggard

LAMAR UNIVERSITY press

ISBN: 978-0-9911074-1-4
Library of Congress Control Number: 2014933866

Manufactured in the United States

Lamar University Press
Beaumont, Texas

for Jim, in all ways

Books from Lamar University Press

Jean Andrews, *High Tides, Low Tides: the Story of Leroy Colombo*
Alan Berecka, *With Our Baggage*
David Bowles, *Flower, Song, Dance: Aztec and Mayan Poetry*
Jerry Bradley, *Crownfeathers and Effigies*
Robert Murray Davis, *Levels of Incompetence: An Academic Life*
Jeffrey Delotto, *Voices Writ in Sand*
Gerald Duff, *Memphis Mojo*
Mimi Ferebee, *Wildfires and Atmospheric Memories*
Ken Hada, *Margaritas and Redfish*
Michelle Hartman, *Disenchanted and Disgruntled*
Dominique Inge, *A Garden on the Brazos*
Gretchen Johnson, *The Joy of Deception*
Tom Mack and Andrew Geyer, editors, *A Shared Voice*
Dave Oliphant, *The Pilgrimage, Selected Poems: 1962-2012*
Janet McCann, *The Crone at the Casino*
Erin Murphy, *Ancilla*
Harold Raley, *Louisiana Rogue*
Carol Coffee Reposa, *Underground Musicians*
Jim Sanderson, *Trashy Behavior*
Jan Seale, *Appearances*
Jan Seale, *The Parkinson Poems*
Melvin Sterne, *The Number You Have Reached*

For information on these and other Lamar Press books go to
www.LamarUniversityPress.Org

Other books by Lynn Hoggard

Sketch of a Serpent (*Ébauche d'un serpent*), translation of a long poem by Paul Valéry
Married to Dance: The Story of Irina and Frank Pal
Tent Posts (Poteaux d'angle), translation of prose poems by Henri Michaux
Nelida, translation of a novel by Countess Marie d'Agoult

Acknowledgments

I am grateful to the editors of these journals and anthologies for publishing some of the pieces in this book:

A Certain Attitude
Clackamus Literary Review
Concho River Review
A Certain Attitude
descant
Helios
New Texas '91
The Texas Anthology
13th Moon
Travois
Xavier Review

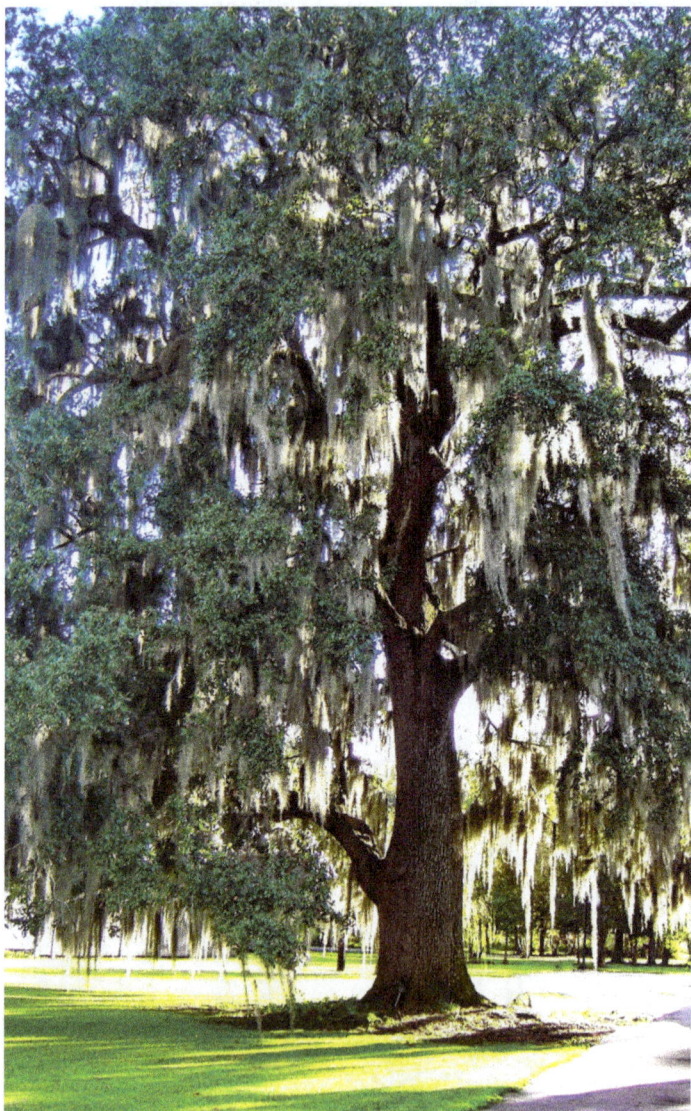
Louisiana Live Oak

CONTENTS

Introduction

I. The Source

II. Eros

III. The Storm's Eye

Introduction

The journey from childhood to adulthood, for many of us, is perilous. If we survive, we may bear scars and even open wounds that ache or cripple us for the rest of our lives. If the journey was joyful, we cherish and celebrate the events and people who helped us know life in its fullness. In either case, these experiences often define who we are as human beings.

For most of us, the journey is both perilous and joyful, as it was for me, and as I've tried to show in these stories and poems about growing up in South Louisiana during the forties, fifties, and sixties. My work as a writer has been to choose which things to tell and to tell them with art and honesty in such a way that they offer more than the random facts of my life. When the magic works, writing can arc into higher meaning, and when it does, it transcends the personal, becoming an artifact of the human spirit.

Because I have written here about places and people who didn't ask to become public, I've changed the names of both. Aside from these changes, the facts and details presented here are true to my memory of them.

I hope you enjoy these stories and poems about growing up in a South Louisiana that was unlike any other time or place. That time and place have now both vanished.

Lynn Hoggard

". . . the distance of their crossing [was] more than a mile"

I. The Source

Louisiana Litany

I saw in Louisiana a live oak growing,
all alone stood it and the moss hung down from the
branches.
> —Walt Whitman

Your hair the greying musk of moss
trailing loose from oak tree to the earth
lair of spiders nest of squirrels
my bed
oh earth my mother

Your arms the branches of a naked tree
withered in an upward stretch
swaying to the rhythms of the slow earth chant
swaying me
oh earth my mother

From your breasts unceasing rain
falling hot on fertile ground
calling chaos from the tangled vegetation
hot on me
oh earth my mother

In your belly swarms the swamp
where womb consumes what it creates
perpetual birth unending death
my source
oh earth my mother

Lynn Hoggard

Your sons the rustling snakes
perfidious servants to your will
my brothers lovers
my life my death
oh earth my mother my mother

Life on the Levee

The six miles to Grandmother LaPlace's house were the road to adventure. For about half the way Cassie and her family headed in their Chevrolet from St. Aimé in a line perpendicular to the Mississippi levee. Once at the tiny community of Burnside, her father turned south down the River Road in the direction of New Orleans, a three-mile stretch to his childhood home that included a steady dribble of houses, a couple of small plantations, and a few clumped settlements along the levee's land side. Just as they made the Burnside turn, however, Cassie and her brother always looked for the monkey, which for years was tethered inside a little shack that had once sheltered a railroad switchman from the elements but now housed a monkey with nothing more to do than react to the passing parade. As they rumbled by, Cassie and her brother leaned out the car window to wave and shout, and the monkey too jumped onto its small window to leap and gesture wildly at them—monkey and kids big-eyed, yelling, and waving to one another. It was their welcome to Grandmother's world.

The settlement where Grandmother lived was called Unity and included a general store, a tiny post office, a large Catholic Church, a strand of houses that faced the levee, and a few dirt roads perpendicular to the river where other houses, many of them unpainted shanties where the black population had lived since the Civil War, lay sprinkled about. Grandmother's house was large, and, like most of the homes along the river, was built atop wide brick pillars rising four

3

John LaPlace after hunting behind his mother's house

or so feet off the ground, with a wide front porch that held a two-seater swing whose chains, as they swayed back and forth, emitted hospitable creaks. Cassie's mother was horrified one day to find Carter and Cassie (then about four and two years old) under Grandmother's house with spoons they had used to shape little dirt "turtles," which they were happily eating. At the time, just at the end of World War II, they lived in an apartment in New Orleans, where their father (who was 4-f because of an irregular heartbeat, making him ineligible to serve in the military) worked as a foreman in a factory that made patrol torpedo boats. Their mother told the family doctor about the dirt-eating, asking his advice. "Leave them alone," he said with a Frenchman's light shrug. "You live upstairs, in the city. They're probably getting nutrients they can't find anywhere else."

Behind Grandmother's house the ample rainwater was collected in a long, metal cistern and, by the time Cassie was six years old, was pumped into the kitchen, but that hadn't always been the case. In the late 40s, the house had no indoor plumbing. The trip to the backyard outhouse, where the children met spiders, intense smells, and the Sears & Roebuck catalog, was not one they'd make alone after dark. For Cassie the trip was perilous even in daytime because of a rooster that chased her whenever she stepped off the back porch. The grownups didn't believe her about the rooster until her uncle happened to be watching one day as it raced shrieking after Cassie, who ran, shrieking also. After that day, she never saw it again, and the joke among the adults was that "Cassie had killed the rooster." She also got a worrisome lesson in natural selection when she saw Grandmother's brood of chickens consistently persecute a young black chick that was lame and seemed to have a skin malady—or perhaps had just been pecked to infection. The flock persisted until it had pecked the chick to death. The pitiless cruelty of it overwhelmed her, but then so did the wringing of the necks of plump hens by Cassie's mother, grandmother, and aunts. The birds' plucked, seared, and steaming bodies later appeared as centerpieces of their sumptuous holiday celebrations, where she didn't bother to make a connection.

At the end of the fenced back yard where the chickens lived was a row of unpainted one-story tumble-down structures, which included a corn crib and a tool shed. They formed a wall of sorts between the house and the wilderness behind. For a short time Cassie enjoyed crawling through the granary of corncobs Grandmother kept for the chickens, until she found herself in the company of several large and irritated rats, whose territory she had invaded.

The fig trees in the yard produced great quantities of sweet, juicy fruit whose milky stem-liquid Cassie's father and brother were allergic to, although they dearly loved figs, so it was her job to climb those trees and pick all the ripe figs she could find to load on their breakfast toast or cereal the following morning. Sometimes they'd just have a bowl of fresh figs in milk.

Behind Grandmother's house, and as far back as any of her young grandchildren could hike, was a narrow strip of land, one of many divided into thin ribbons of riverfront

Grandmother LaPlace's birthday

property. The lot facing the levee was perhaps one hundred feet wide, but it extended behind the house for two or three miles. These were the woods where Cassie's grandfather, who had died before she was born, her father, and his three brothers had hunted game, and it was also where the six or eight grandkids, gathered on their Sunday-afternoon visits, would explore for snakes, possums, raccoons, rabbits, and any other wild thing they could find. When they needed to rest, to avoid the stinging nettles that thrived in the grass around them, they'd climb a fallen tree and tell each other snippets of children's wisdom, including that humans weren't brought by storks, no siree, her cousin had said; his father told him he'd hatched from an egg, like a chicken.

The part of the levee that faced Grandmother's house, the land side, was the children's playground. The side facing the Mississippi was off limits to them, but they made little forays into it to seek treasures like broken shrimp cages, innards of cleaned fish that they poked with sticks, and debris of all kinds, including driftwood, old nets, and even animal bones—a special treasure—left by other animals or by the river's rise and fall. Cassie would look at the water's vastness and think of what her father had told her—that he and his brothers had learned to swim there. When they reached the age of twelve, they swam all the way across. Since the river had strong currents and an unpredictable undertow, they had to favor its strength and swim at an angle, which made the distance of their crossing more than a mile. Cassie was impressed. To her they were gods.

On the kids' side of the levee they'd sometimes haul

cardboard boxes to the top and push off with one foot as they hopped inside. The box would usually careen down the slope at a dangerous and exciting angle, unless it sputtered like a spent firecracker, coming to a sad little halt as some other kid whished by with a yelp of victory. Sometimes the box flipped over, leaving them scratched and bleeding, their clothes smeared with grass stains so stubborn to remove that their mothers said they were going to forbid the box races but never did.

If they were lucky enough to have a nickel, they'd head for Robichaux's grocery, just next to Grandmother's house on the north side. Cracker Jacks were Cassie's favorite, not only because of the crunchy sweetness of the caramel popcorn but also because of the little prize waiting at the bottom —a plastic ring, a whistle, or maybe a tiny plastic acrobat on a stand.

Once, though, when the Robichaux's daughter had gone up the levee with them and after they'd bought their candy and were eating it, she asked if they wanted to see a crazy girl. Of course they did. Her furtive manner told them she wasn't supposed to be doing this, so she had to sneak them into her house, which connected directly from the back of the store and continued on an upper floor. She led them outside, however, to a back entrance and up a flight of stairs. They walked on tiptoe down the hall and into a large room whose door the girl held open, a room empty for about half its depth and semi-dark from only one small window placed high on the south wall; the room's other half had bars its full width, some kind of mattress on the floor, and, sitting on the mattress and making noises in their direction was a girl about Cassie's age. Her features displayed what Cassie later would call severe mental retardation—a low brow that sloped back, a broad, flat nose, a wide face—but back then she didn't know those things. The Robichaux girl relished the other children's shock at her sister, who became increasingly agitated by their presence and began to rock from side to side, beat against the bars with her head and hands, and make deep, gurgling sounds in her throat. Fearing her parents would hear, her sister abruptly made them leave. Terrified and deeply disturbed, Cassie thought the girl would have killed them if she had gotten free. For months she had tangled dreams about the girl's wild eyes, her animal moves, her gurgling throat, her caged and desperate existence. Her family probably had nowhere to take her; they dealt with her as they could.

It was an insulated and isolated community. Cassie's father had gone hundreds of miles north to college at Louisiana Tech in Ruston, where he played baseball and basketball on athletic scholarships and met Cassie's mother, who was majoring in home economics because that was the only field her father would allow a young woman to study. They eloped December 6, 1941. "We married one day," her mother said, "and war was declared the next."

But the home-front wars weren't just between the two of them. When Cassie's father's parents learned that their son had married outside the Catholic faith, they didn't allow her mother inside their house until the couple had been properly married by a priest. Her mother offered to become

Catholic if the new family could attend church together, but Cassie's father said he had already had enough church for a lifetime—including a half-dozen years as an acolyte—and wasn't going back except to visit. Her mother took the children to the Methodist church instead—to those in settlements around St. Aimé until she finally founded one of her own, the first Methodist church in their town. Nevertheless, each of the four children was baptized by a priest in the Catholic Church at Unity, "so their souls will be saved," Grandmother said, nodding gravely. She often drew them aside one at a time during visits to ask them to attend church with her; or she would ask them to make their First Communion in the Catholic Church—requests that drove Cassie's mother to distraction. Her father would neither support his wife's anger nor ask his mother to stop evangelizing. "I've had many more problems over religion with your Daddy's family than I ever had with your Daddy," Cassie's mother told her.

When Cassie stayed with her grandmother, she often walked with her the winding half-mile along the levee to church, particularly to late-afternoon Mass, where she was dazzled by statues that glittered in the sun's tilting rays, by the incense, the chanting choir, and the manifold ceremonial tasks—such as making the sign of the Cross on one's head, chest, and shoulders with Holy Water and genuflecting toward the altar before entering the pew. Grandmother sat beside her but in another world, moving her fingers through the beads of her rosary as her lips moved, sometimes silently, sometimes chanting along with the priest and other congregants: "Holy Mary, Mother of God, pray for us, sinners now and at the hour of our death. Amen." This was Grandmother's second mass of the day. Each morning she attended six o'clock services as well.

She was a petite woman with deeply hooded brown eyes, a dark, tight bun at the base of her neck, and the mannerisms of a bird. Her father, a carpenter, had immigrated to Louisiana from France in 1874, and she still spoke French fluently. She never raised her voice or appeared angry, but anger must certainly have been within her, considering her harsh behavior toward Cassie's mother. Instead, she withdrew into a quiet, safe place inside herself or her church, where meanings were orderly and clear. Her husband, a Welshman by descent, had been a rowdy sort, a railroad switchman who spent his spare time in the ways of the region—hunting, fishing, drinking, and playing cards. He left family matters to his wife, who formed a snug cocoon that enveloped herself, her children, and her church.

The grandest moments of church on the levee, however, came on Christmas Eve, with Midnight Mass. All the relatives who could—sometimes nearly thirty of them—squeezed into Grandmother's house for the day and night, where they'd sleep on mattresses stuffed with Spanish moss. After they'd laid their dozens of gifts around the tree and enjoyed an evening meal and extended storytelling, they made their way on foot near midnight to the church, the children nodding with sleep or carried in their parents' arms, sometimes sound asleep. The air held a damp chill, often with mist falling. Spaced along the levee at several hundred-yard intervals were giant bonfires, like huge river candles, which had been lighted at nightfall. Children on the levee side ran and played around the steaming embers as the pilgrims on the other side moved slowly toward the church. Once inside the warm and brightly lighted building they listened to Christmas anthems roll down from the choir loft; then the priest intoned—in a Latin that echoed against the walls and the high ceiling—*Dei plena sunt Omnia*—all things are filled with God.

Martha LaPlace soon after her marriage

Lynn Hoggard

Port-a-Potty

Cassie's bottom forms a perfect circle because of the little round pot on which she spent the greater part of her early childhood.

Her mother, whose will was ferocious, believed that to yield to a child for any reason signaled incompetence to be a parent, so the LaPlace kids regularly cried themselves to sleep and, after everyone else had left, sat at the dinner table hour after hour malevolently eyeing their Brussel sprouts. Potty training was no different.

Cassie's older brother Carter breezed through it as though he'd practiced in another life. Once there and told to produce, he worked like a vending machine: food in, poot out. Then came Cassandra. Since one of her names was Mary, she heard many times the nursery rhyme, "Mary, Mary, quite contrary"; she may have tended in that direction, but the rhyme drove her straight there, with a constitution stuck on stubborn. Once on the pot, her system locked down. From time to time she'd rise a bit to check, in case some miracle had happened. The rule, of course, was that she couldn't go play until she'd done something significant, so many a day went by that she sat on the pot from breakfast until lunch, whining and crying and occasionally cheating when she thought she could get away with a quick run around the room. Every now and then her mother would let her toddle off, leaving the pot empty, but such dispensations were rare.

Children, however, are resourceful, and so was Cassie.

As she neared the age of two, she perfected a trick that allowed her an astonishing freedom and redefined her life: Holding the pot by its lip snugly to her bottom, she'd stretch her legs forward, then pull them to her, sliding the pot and herself smoothly along—st-r-e-t-c-h and then pull. Aside from the inconvenience of doorsills, which required a little hop and a mounding glide, she could go virtually anywhere—and did.

Decades later, Cassie's Uncle Barry reminded her how she used to be all over his house on that pot—no one knew where. He said his favorite memory was the time during Thanksgiving dinner when Cassie and that pot suddenly shot out from under their dining table and sped off to another room.

"You looked like an inchworm," he grinned, "hot-roddin' it on a bottle cap!"

Carter and Cassie

Lynn Hoggard

Bug in My Cereal

"You look like an aardvark!"

"No, *you* look like a...a arkvark!"

Cassie was three. Her five-year-old brother, Carter, sat across from her at the breakfast table, which was surrounded by a cozy wooden booth in their kitchen at the rear of their shotgun-style duplex. They were having oatmeal again, a cereal whose slimy consistency isn't for the squeamish, and Cassie was squeamish. Her mother, who taught school, was often in a hurry to get the children fed and to the Cajun neighbor-lady's house, where they'd stay until their mother came home at the end of the school day. Sometimes the oatmeal had lumps in it, which Cassie learned later came from its being cooked too quickly, but at the time all she knew was that the minute her tongue felt a lump, a gag reflex kicked in, and the cereal held the horror of a bowl of bugs.

Her mother, though, was stern on discipline and was not put off by horror. Cassie would postpone, dawdle, whine, but she couldn't leave the table until she had finished her oatmeal, gagging her way through. When she hadn't finished it before time for her mother to leave, she was escorted next door along with her bowl of cereal, and Mrs. Boudreaux was told that Cassie could not go outside to play until she finished her breakfast.

So oatmeal and Cassie had a charged relationship. Her brother didn't help matters. In her infancy Cassie had tyrannized him, her mother said, crawling around maliciously to break his toys. He was forbidden to retaliate because Cassie

14

Cassie and Carter with Martha

was his little sister. Now that she was older, he looked for chinks through which he could exact revenge. This particular morning she sat mournfully before her oatmeal, loathe to put the first gummy spoonful in her mouth. Carter, who was eyeing her with a strange glint, suddenly leaned from where he sat and scooped a dead cockroach, which he must have spied earlier—and dropped it in her oatmeal, quickly stirring the ghastly mixture with Cassie's spoon.

"Aieeeeeee!" she shrieked, banging her heels against the booth.

Her mother rushed over, already angry, to ask what was wrong.

"Carter put a bug in my cereal!" Cassie screamed. Meanwhile, Carter was busily eating his own oatmeal, seeming preoccupied with other thoughts.

"Cassie, eat your oatmeal," her mother said sternly.

"No-o-o-o-o-o," Cassie cried. "It's got a bug in it!"

"Cassie, you heard me. I don't have time for your foolishness. Eat your cereal, or you'll get a spanking!"

Either way, she was doomed. She suddenly knew what it meant to have two bad choices, so, being three, she dissolved into hysterical sobs.

Sobs so hysterical, apparently, that they frightened her mother. Cassie was too young to understand how authentic behavior often carries the authority of truth. Her mother took Cassie in her arms and tried to comfort her, but all Cassie could see in her imagination was that horrific, goo-infested vermin crawling toward her, whiskers dripping slime. She screamed, her mother said, for a long time, and it wasn't until her mother scraped Cassie's cereal in the dog's bowl that she saw the cockroach.

At which point Carter got the spanking meant for Cassie.

"Daddy gone pitchin'. . ."

Runaway, Age Three

Daddy gone pitchin'
his baseball game
lef' me at home
Mama washin' my hair
nowhere near Daddy

Daddy gone pitchin'
his baseball game
lef' fluffin' my hair in the sun
sittin' on the front-porch steps
cryin'

Daddy gone pitchin'
his baseball game
lef' me alone
wantin' Daddy—

    now I be gone too

The bayou across the way

Lynn Hoggard

A Learning

> *But I say to you, love your enemies....*
> —Matthew 5:44

Miz Boudreaux kept on beating her,
the four-year-old, who dangled
by the one left arm she grabbed
to yank her off the front porch swing.
Miz Boudreaux yelled,
Evil chil', evil! sweet-singin'
abou' de devil an's to how you love 'im—
Give you a learnin', devil chil'!

Miz Boudreaux kept on
swinging back and forth her sure right arm
across the blond-haired, bobbing form
whose cries were all of Sunday school
and loving enemies—even Satan—
now swelling for the world to hear

Where no one did
but a few black snakes across the way,
tucked in mud at the bayou's edge.
They writhed, then opened cotton mouths,
closing them again
around a glimpse
of white.

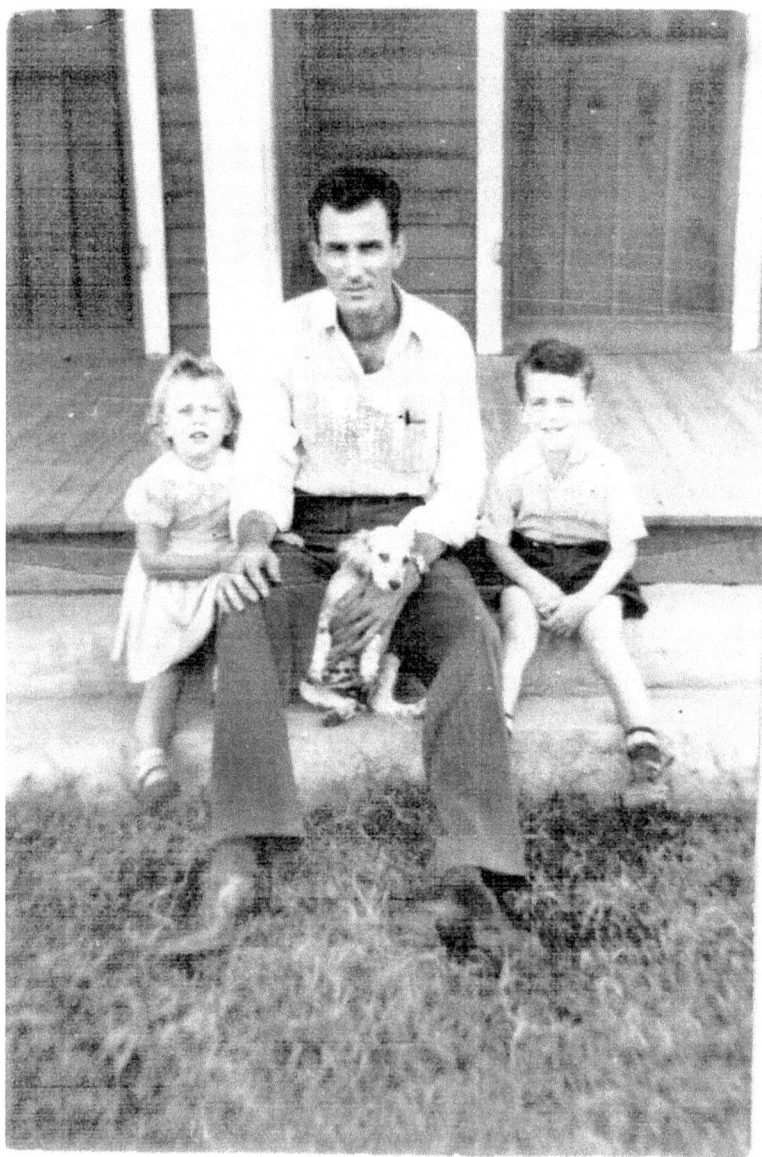
Cassie, John LaPlace, Carter, and puppy

God's Will

She was Cassie's beautifullest paper doll, her own Betty Grable, made of heavy cardboard and permanently imprinted with a sexy, white strapless swimsuit, blonde up-swept hair, and long, pretty legs. Five-year-old Cassie with her scissors had clipped Betty's paper dresses from the square sheets they were imprinted on. Using her tongue for help, she carefully turned the paper this way and that to make sure the fold-back tabs didn't tear as she curved around them. She wanted the clothes to fit perfectly, so that everything about Betty would be perfect—as perfect as Betty was.

Most important of all Betty's clothes, however, was the green lamé strapless evening gown Cassie had just finished cutting out. It had the sheen of silver where the light touched it suggestively, at the fullness of the hips and across the breasts. That gown sang, it beckoned, it cooed. Sitting on the kitchen floor, Cassie couldn't stop touching it, turning it this way, that way, imagining conversations as the gown turned to address its admirers:

"Of course, you may get me a glass of water," the gown said to a handsome stranger just beyond the cache of cut-outs, next to where Betty herself was waiting expectantly to be dressed.

"Pick it up!" another voice interjected, much sterner and more forceful. The gown, as if trying to translate these words into a language it could understand, stopped moving and adopted a puzzled, sideways air.

"I said, pick it up, Cassie," the voice repeated, now more insistently. Startled, Cassie looked up from where Betty lay and saw her father, home from work, standing above her, six feet and three inches above the floor, insisting that Betty and all her lovely clothes be tossed into a hasty and undignified pile, where Betty would be pushed away from life, from happiness, from the love that bloomed between herself and Cassie.

"God told me not to," Cassie replied without hesitation, looking fixedly at Betty, her voice projecting an authority that tried to match her father's own. She sat her ground, protecting Betty, her clothes, and her small world.

Like a mighty hawk, he swooped, her father, grabbing the green lamé gown in his talons and ripping it in two at its shapely waist, dropping the pieces before Cassie's astonished eyes. If he had ripped her heart from her chest, she could not have been more amazed. Or ruined.

Tears welled in her eyes as she looked into her father's implacable and now very angry face. He repeated, "I said, pick it up!"

Her chest heaved as she pushed the heaps of paper into a pile. Finally she stood up, head down, wads of paper pressed against her chest.

"Now what did God tell you?" her father asked, a hostile edge to his voice.

"He told me to pick 'em up," she said in a little voice, walking away.

Laughing Ladies

was the game
Mary and I called our lip-to-lip
belly-button-on-button stand
there on the big swing
by the honeysuckle vines
Our knees would bump
and pump, bump and pump
us higher

higher we'd soar
above the gumball tree
wiggling like polliwogs
against a wave of giggles
Little girls becoming
laughing ladies

in the arc of air
the chill of sweat
the breathless breaths
We swayed on a slender rope
into the roller-coasting groin-thrill
we knew would come

and with it
came the laughing—
circus-fat-lady
laughing!

Cassie, Carter, and pony

Stoned by Catholics

Cassie saw being Protestant as a dark cloud over her life. In a profoundly Catholic community, priests felt secure of their monopoly on religious truth. Protestants of every stripe, along with the godless—a combined total of only a couple of hundred among the nearly one thousand Catholics —were simply called "non-Catholics," as if such groups were unworthy of their own name. The rural nature of South Louisiana led people to favor what joined them, and what joined the vast majority was Catholicism.

Cassie remembered later on in high school being told by a boy she adored that his parents would not let him date her, a non-Catholic. Maybe he was making excuses. They apparently did let him date a girl known at St. Aimé High School as "bed-legs"— beloved, Cassie guessed, of both God and man. And, once, a girlfriend reported to her that the nuns had said that non-Catholics engaged in bestiality. "What's that?" Cassie asked. When the friend explained, somewhat crudely, Cassie was appalled and felt sullied that the idea had even passed through her head. She told her friend that she hadn't seen any Protestants do that, but the friend stuck to her nuns' story.

The most vivid experience of her Protestantism, how-ever, came when she was about seven. She and her brother Carter were walking the several blocks home from school when they heard shuffling behind them. A group of kids, maybe six or eight of them, about their own age, had gathered and was moving in their direction. They were talking among themselves and looking malevolently at Cassie and Carter. The pair turning toward them must have triggered something, because one of them yelled, "You goin' to Hell!"

The group wasn't clear about their intentions and apparently hadn't thought through their plan. Almost aimlessly they began to pick up rocks and dirt and, in a kind of petulant awkwardness, started throwing them at Cassie and Carter. The two started running, a movement that triggered a reflex—the thrill of the chase—and within seconds Carter and Cassie were being pelted with rocks and dirt from the group rushing after them, now screaming, "Non-Catholics!", "Go to Hell!", "You go to Hell, you heah!" Not having much vocabulary, they kept saying the same things.

If they had caught the pair, things might have gone badly, but by now Carter and Cassie were home. They raced to the back door, which was always unlocked and where the gang didn't dare follow. When their mother saw their nicks and cuts, she was not only alarmed but enraged. Her fighting nature was never more deeply stirred than when a wrong needed righting or a child needed protection. When those two were joined, as they were here, she became a fire-breathing Crusader, going from principal to priest to mayor to police.

Carter and Cassie were never stoned again, by Catholics or anyone else. They now knew, however, more fully than ever before, just how outside their community they were.

Lynn Hoggard

Child of a Different Place

Pretty Veda Arceneaux resided
with her kin in an abandoned bus
in woods beside a swamp; her mom decided
she should go to school without more fuss.

Her skin was white, her eyes were green; her hair,
which curled around her oval face, was black
and thick and full of lice. She was more fair
than any child, in dresses made of sack.

Contraried, Veda Arceneaux left home
and disliked school. A shy and untamed thing,
she wouldn't learn. Not wanting to belong,
she drifted back to what the swamp would bring.

Hilda's Unluck

I ain't had much luck shine down on me:
Men-gitis when I was a baby
lef' me with this hump here on my back,
so I had to walk both front- and sideways
makin' like I didn't feel the spitballs
or rocks a-hittin' me when recess came.

Then I got some more unluck one day
when a bunch of boys yelled *Crip!*
and pushed me down them concrete steps,
where I laid cryin', more broke up than before.
I cain't reckon why their hearts went meaner
than that stone, so cold upside my face.

"[They] pushed me down them concrete steps"

MARTHA AND MARY

"Clickety-clackety-clickety!" chattered the Singer sewing machine whose little foot danced while the needle stitched the white satin fabric Martha was feeding it bit by bit. She skillfully folded under the material's raw edge, forming a smooth hemline that wouldn't fray. "Too much work, too much!" she told her mechanical helper as she pressed her leg against the lever to increase the speed. The machine trotted ahead, leaving behind an impeccable dotted line of fine, white thread that, finally, traced its half-circle and pulled to a rest. "There!" Martha said as she snipped the thread and held the satin half-skirt to the sunlight to be sure the stitching was straight, with no unwanted pleats. "Perfect!" she congratulated herself; then she quickly stitched the front half of the skirt to its identical back portion, making the circle complete. In spite of the pressure she felt to hurry, she smiled in satisfaction.

The gown would be splendid. She had first cut tiny patterns from tissue paper, using as her model measurements from Mary Cassandra's doll Carol. Then she had bought the fabrics—satin, lace, tulle, and tiny flowers for the wedding gown; a beige-and-white wool print with tiny buttons for the slacks and matching jacket; white taffeta for a majorette's uniform with green and gold bars of color across its chest, and a half-yard of filmy light-blue nylon for a nightgown topped by a pink peignoir to drape over it that, when layered, created a shifting, dreamy, rainbow effect, like water in sunshine. For each outfit, in addition to buying fabrics and designing and cutting patterns, Martha had used her trusty Singer with the skill of a professional. Quickly and flawlessly, outfit by outfit, she stitched her designs together. Today was December twenty-first. She had finished everything but the wedding gown, with its white-tulle ruffle that would cascade down the gown's front from waistline to hem, interspersed with bouquets of tiny silken flowers that she would stitch by hand. Martha was severely limited in the time she could work on these clothes, not only by her teaching job and household duties, but also because she couldn't let her seven-year-old daughter see any of this. The wardrobe was Mary Cassie's gift from Santa and would be a surprise.

Wiping sweat from her forehead, Martha thought for the umpteenth time how fiendishly difficult it was to do all that she did—teach full time, be mother (and often father, too) to four children, be a wife and social companion to her husband, be the secretary-treasurer of the Methodist church, and officer in half a dozen other groups and clubs, in addition to continuing her post-graduate studies at a nearby university in order to be able, one day, to qualify for an administrative position in the public school system. Weekends, like today, were an endless chain of heavy cleaning and cooking; Sundays involved Sunday school and church followed by her cooking and serving the biggest meal of the week. Weekdays were even worse. She was exhausted by the time she came home at four in the afternoon, yet she still had clothes that hung on the outdoors line that needed to be gathered, folded, and put away, and dinner to prepare and then the clean-up. She sometimes would lay her head down

Martha LaPlace got very little help

for a minute, just for a minute—as she was doing right now on the Singer's sturdy frame—to allow the fatigue to pool inside her. The minute it did, she popped defiantly back up. She would finish the wardrobe! She didn't have money to buy clothes for Mary Cassie's doll, and, anyway, she could make even more attractive clothes than the store-bought ones. It was time that lacked, energy that flagged, if she let herself give in to those villains.

She could design and make the clothes herself, Martha thought, smiling wryly, because she had majored in home economics in college—something she hadn't wanted to do but that was required by her father, a strong disciplinarian and their town's chief of police, if she wanted to go to college at all: "No daughter of mine has any business in college unless it's to make herself a better wife and mother," he stated emphatically. Majoring in home-ec, she had nevertheless acquired a college degree, or at least had begun one when World War II came down like a machete on her life. Just beginning her second year of college, she and her boyfriend had eloped. Once she had children, she went back to college at night and during summer until she earned her undergraduate degree in education. By then, she had a taste for learning, and she kept on going, despite fatigue and pressure. It was her lifeline to a better future. None of it had been easy, she reminded herself, and it certainly wasn't now.

She got very little help from her own side of the family, who thought she was full of hot and fiery dreams of status and power that none of them had needed for their own happiness; or from her husband, who seemed now only to want a woman to warm his bed, cook his food, and care for his children while he raced home from work to escape, as fully as possible, to the woods for hunting, the bayous for fishing, or the back rooms of the night clubs sprinkled along the levee, where he could shoot pool or play poker; or from her husband's family, who saw her, an uppity Protestant, as some kind of deviant—half Martin Luther, ready to nail her theses to their church doors, and half Jean-Jacques Rousseau with his eye-rolling craziness about education and child-rearing—but worse—she wore a skirt and produced multiple little non-Catholics; and, sadly, she didn't even get help from her own children, who, probably because she worked so hard and did so much for them, were growing up passive, lazy, and less intelligent than she had been at their age—she who had received, according to her high-school principal, the highest IQ in the history of Watertight, Louisiana! When she thought about her own childhood as the daughter of a mother confined to a wheelchair, she was peppered by so many memories of projects she had initiated in church, school, and home that it almost seemed as if these children were from an alien gene pool. If she thought it would help, she would have shaken them by the shoulders until their parts hooked up and worked properly.

Thinking these things, Martha didn't notice that Mary Cassie had quietly entered the room. The doll's wedding gown was spread, partially finished, on the bed behind the sewing machine, in the direction that faced Mary Cassie. As Martha was about to snatch the dress away, she glanced at her daughter to see if she had noticed it. She had. Her blue eyes were huge with amazement. "A wedding gown..! Who's it for, Mama?" she asked.

"Well, your Aunt Jewel asked if I would make this dress for your cousin Barbara's doll for Christmas, and I said yes," Martha answered matter-of-factly, not looking at Mary Cassie and appearing busy and almost angry as she hastily tossed the dress, along with thread, pincushion, braid, and snaps into a small, round box that she placed on the top shelf of her closet.

A long moment passed. As she processed this news, Mary Cassie's small shoulders sagged, her eyes veiled over, and her chin trembled. Saying nothing, she turned and walked toward her room. Martha felt a kind of nausea, both of dread and irritation, in the pit of her stomach. She didn't want to hurt the child, but what was she to do? It was for her that she was working so hard, feeling so tired. Why did she have to walk in so sneakily that Martha didn't even know she was there?

A moment later, folding the day's laundry, an image of Mary Cassie's drooping shoulders welled inside her, making Martha feel small and mean. Just as she had always fought off criticism in the past, from others or herself, she resisted letting the feeling take control. Mary Cassie was such a difficult child, full of strange moods and needs, brooding and soulful, always in some daydream. Martha couldn't fathom how the child could sit placidly for hours, drawing her little pictures, telling herself stories as she drew, or sometimes singing bits of songs she made up—such silly things! A thought came to her that Martha had had many times before:

how much more fun it would have been to have a daughter like herself, filled with projects and activities, sassy and endlessly resourceful, always ready to tackle every new challenge, and determined never, ever to be defeated by an obstacle. This strange, amorphous creature left her puzzled and paralyzed.

Nevertheless, she tiptoed slowly through the hall that led to Mary Cassie's bedroom, where, outside the door, she could hear muffled sobs. For a moment, pity surged inside her. Just as she was about to rush into the bedroom, take the child in her arms, and tell her—what would she tell her?—tell her Santa would certainly know to bring dresses for her own doll!—she stopped. The surprise would be diminished if Mary Cassie expected it. All that work—for what? It would be commissioned labor. Those dresses needed to be totally unexpected, a marvelous gift from Santa.

As she returned to the laundry that still needed folding, Martha wondered again about the child's tears, about whether her present unhappiness might dampen the pleasure she would feel when she saw the four perfect doll outfits beneath the Christmas tree. Would she know how much she was loved? Should Martha go back?

"No," she told herself, shaking the notion from her head as she picked up a pair of Mary Cassie's overalls and briskly folded them. "It's a huge gift. She'll know!"

Lynn Hoggard

Over the Top

   of our almost finished strawberry-icebox pie,
we were spraying, Mama and I,
whipped cream from a can that gurgled and spat
a clotted, fluffy moon

   when all at once the can
leaped snarling out of Mama's hand
and spewed milk swirls on walls, floor, ceiling, air,
on Mama and me

   while we laughed and chased the crazed
wall-writing moon-calf round the room,
slipped in his drool,
and finally grabbed him, held him tight

   as he hacked a final moon chunk up—
and died.

Chuh

As an eighth grader in the St. Aimé, Louisiana, school system, Cassie had the humiliating task of taking English in a class taught by her mother. For most of the year she looked fixedly at her desktop, listening but not lifting her eyes during discussions or as explanations were given. One day, however, she raised her head in spite of herself.

The students had been assigned an in-class writing. All heads were bent over sheets of paper as pencils scribbled. Then it came:

"Hey, Miz LaPlace, 'ow you spell *chuh*?"

Cassie's head snapped up, eyes wide.

It was Calvin Melançon, one of the Cajun boys, his arm held straight in the air with a sense of urgent purpose. Cassie's mother, from non-Cajun north Louisiana, looked at him blankly.

"*Chuh*?" she asked.

"*Chuh*," he repeated. "'ow you spell it?"

"I don't know, Calvin," she said. "Why don't you use it in a sentence?"

"Aw right," he obliged, laying down his pencil. His hands, like those of a bandleader, led the way, shaping themselves into something like a catcher's mitt: "You playin' baseball wid de boyz, an' de udda boy, he got de ball, an' you wan' it, so you say, 'Hey, man, trrow it *chuh*'!"

"Calvin," her mother said, her mouth twisting slightly, "that's spelled h-e-r-e."

"Eh?" he asked, incredulous.

33

"H-e-r-e."

"Aw right," he nodded agreeably with a little shrug, retrieving his pencil. As a Cajun, he already knew about the difference between his world and their world. If asked, he was perfectly willing to bridge that gap with an absurdity.

Squeaky

An Offering

Relations between blacks and whites in 1950s South Louisiana were as fused as they were sometimes cruel. Given the cultural richness of the region, which could have been affirmed and celebrated, those in power often chose instead to condemn and exclude on the basis of difference, as if their side alone held the truth. When Cassie said to her mother, pointing to a black person on the sidewalk in front of them, "Look, Mama, that lady's wearing socks with her high heels," her mother gave her hand a little jerk and replied, "That's not a lady, that's a woman." Yet her mother also helped integrate the schools and worked throughout her life to help people in need, from the homeless at their door to the shut-ins on the far side of town.

When Cassie one day saw boys in the hall of her high school elbowing each other, then guffawing and snickering, she asked her brother, who had been standing within earshot, what they were talking about. "They call it 'nigger-knockin'," he said, explaining that on weekends at night, five or six boys would pile into a car with the windows rolled down, carrying baseball bats and targeting any black who happened to be walking on the side of the road.

Sheltered in childhood even from knowledge of such things, Cassie's experience with the black race was contained in a single person—Maggie Lawson—who worked for the six-member LaPlace family for more than a decade, cleaning, washing, ironing, and doing other household chores. On the four days a week when Cassie's mother had the car, she drove to the black part of town to pick up Maggie, who waited in a rocker on the front porch of her unpainted shotgun house. But on the day that Cassie's father, who carpooled with four other people, drove the family car to Baton Rouge, Maggie had to walk the three miles each way to and from their house, whatever the season or weather.

She weighed more than two hundred pounds and waddled painfully. She usually wore a bandana around her hair, which was a mottled black and grey. She was maybe in her late forties when she began working for the family and already then had grown children, but Cassie didn't know whether she had a husband and, if so, where he was. When after about ten years Maggie could no longer work because of her health, Cassie's mother continued to give Maggie money and clothes, but her life must have been harder than a rock. Cassie was ashamed to admit that, once she left for college, she didn't know what became of Maggie Lawson.

Cassie had other things she was ashamed of regarding Maggie, including the fact that she sometimes put clothes to wash that weren't actually dirty and could have been worn again because she wanted them starched and ironed freshly, a chore that Maggie did, standing up, hour after steaming hour, in their house. Her disposition was placid, stoic, and gentle. Cassie's mother called her lazy, but then she called Cassie lazy, too, along with anyone who wasn't on fire with purposeful energy.

When Cassie was ten, she discovered one morning when she went to feed him that her pet flying squirrel had died. She and Maggie were alone in the house, and Cassie began to sob, holding Squeaky, cold and stiff and utterly changed, still curled inside the little round powder box that was his bed. Cassie cradled the squirrel and wept, while Maggie rocked Cassie in her arms, whispering over and over in her ear, "It's go' be aw'right, honey, it's go' be aw'right"—until it almost was. When Cassie calmed down, Maggie returned to her work.

Much later, Cassie realized that she'd never thanked Maggie for this kindness. In her memory it glows with unearthly light: an offering of pure, uncomplicated love—a little like the grace of God.

Church Lady

Cassie became Church Lady when her mother anointed her Founding Janitor of St. Aimé's Kelleher Memorial Methodist Church. A few years before that, her mother had persuaded a wealthy widow to underwrite the cost of building the town's first Methodist church. It became the place where the then twenty-five-member congregation gathered every Sunday and the place that Cassie cleaned every Saturday for nearly seven years, from the time she was twelve until she went to north Louisiana for college. Not only did she clean the church and, a few years later, the Sunday school building that was built beside it; she was also, at one time or other, church pianist and organist (when the church acquired an organ), choir director, Sunday school teacher, and president of the Methodist Youth Fellowship. She could even remember at about the age of eight being awarded a medal for a year of perfect attendance, and, each year after that, when she had fifty-two weeks of perfection, she received a little bar to dangle beneath that medal. Before she left for college—when she stopped going to church altogether —she was ten times perfect.

The cleaning chores were drudgery that Cassie hated, but she knew better than to slack off because, otherwise, she would have to listen to her mother during the family's Sunday fried-chicken dinner—condor-eyed in her surveillance of Cassie's work—recite her sins and omissions. "I had to brush the dust off my knees when I stood up from the Communion rail," she might say, looking skyward with a sense of injured dignity, "and Bobbie Bourke actually came up to me after church to say that the offering plates had dust on them." Part of the problem was that it took Cassie three hours to do a decent job vacuuming, dusting, and straightening both buildings, and, when there was a problem, such as a toilet running in the Sunday school restroom, she spent time figuring it out and fixing it; then she had to rush to be ready when her mother or, a few years later, her brother picked her up in the car at the appointed time. Another problem was the dreaming. If she found something during her cleaning—an earring, maybe—it might send her on an extended reverie—which, like an enchantment, slowed all of her movements—about who might have been wearing it, how well the woman may have treasured it, and even where it might have been kept in her house (in a box she kept hidden, maybe, with gold embroidery on it?). It had to go, of course, in the little lost box at the church entrance.

But there were things Cassie loved about being Church Lady. She felt that, there, she was in a quietly magical place; alone, she sometimes sang out loud as she worked—pop tunes ("Teen Angel," "In the Still of the Night"), hymns ("Follow the Gleam," "Are Ye Able?"), folk songs ("Flying Trapeze," "Ben Bolt"), or even country music ("Four Walls," "Irene, Goodnight")—in a guileless way that would have seemed addled to a chance listener, but the singing let her go places where, strangely, joy was overflowing. Why she went there as Church Lady and not at other times was a mystery she didn't explore. She simply knew that, there, the labor and solitude brought happiness.

She remembered one time in particular at about the age of ten when, not in church, she had discovered almost by accident how to add another self to her personality. The discovery, which started as a game, showed her that she could summon this identity through will and imagination. That day, feeling listless and unwell before a piano lesson, Cassie was stung to the quick by a criticism from her mother —something about her having no drive. After that, she wasn't about to say that she didn't feel well, so she walked the usual half-mile to her lesson—crossing the railroad bridge high above the sleepy bayou meandering below—as she dreamed up a game of pretend, pretending that right now, for example, she felt fine in order to see how she could function while feeling awful. The worse she felt during that lesson, the harder she pretended, and the harder she pretended, the more she tried to play the music well—Robert Schumann's "Träumerei," his reverie. Hot and aching, she stretched into his yearning that arced across octaves of pain and sadness and then, become a pure and trembling liquid, poured itself into sweetness and beauty. She felt it, she knew it, she was living his dream and pressing to weave it into the notes she played. Her teacher, Miss Virgie Bourgeois, who, in her lace-up shoes, sat beside Cassie on the piano bench, must have seen something in her flushed face or glassy eye that made her touch Cassie's forehead with her hand, which she drew back quickly. A few minutes later she was coming toward Cassie with a thermometer, and a few minutes after that she was driving Cassie home, where she told her mother that Cassie's temperature was 104 degrees. She couldn't understand it, Miss Virgie said, shaking her head in bewilderment; that had been one of Cassie's best lessons. "I was *trying*," Cassie thought.

"You're an unusual person," Miss Virgie told her years later, when at fifteen Cassie was graduating from her instruction. "I don't think I ever reached the deeper part of you, but I think I glimpsed in you the seeds of greatness." A little dazzled, Cassie had to admit that Miss Virgie's words left room for doubt: "Possible seeds," she reminded herself.

The church cleaning was lonely drudgery, but its hard and happy solitude taught Cassie discipline and perseverance —skills that served her well. She learned, in fact, that when she could control and direct her dreaming she could achieve things. And from that recognition—along with the knowledge that she had, if she needed it, a second self in reserve—she understood that she had better be clear about what she wanted, because once she focused on a goal, she would almost always reach it. Sometimes the prize was insubstantial, like winning a beauty contest or the heart of the wrong boy. She had better be sure.

The Village Idiot

Back then, every village had its idiot, and theirs was no different, as Cassie could attest. Babe belonged to St. Aimé and behaved as if St. Aimé belonged to him. Maybe it did. Someone, or several people, must have taken care of him, since year after year he received food, clothes, and shelter. When Cassie was still a child, Babe was already a grown man, but it was hard to tell whether he was in his twenties or his forties, since he had little hair, and his swarthy skin had neither wrinkles nor freshness. No one appeared to know where he lived. He often sat on someone's back steps during the day or lurched through the streets, looking around with wild-eyed impudence. His clothes, always haphazard combinations of plaids, stripes, or checks, were a notch shy of ragged. He talked in raspy, broken phrases, the words not fully formed, as if his tongue had fallen asleep. Some could make out "I do' know" and "Dass righ'," but sometimes they were mystified. Used to being teased or taunted, Babe became excited when asked to repeat, so when people didn't understand him the first time, they tended to ignore him as he lurched behind them, repeating himself.

He was water boy during home football games, and the crowd often cheered—"Go, Babe, go!"—as he struggled onto the field with his bucket of water. He seemed to love the attention and would sometimes wave to the crowd, smiling broadly, as he returned to the sidelines.

Everyone said he was harmless, but Cassie knew better. That knowledge came as she and her friend Beth

Colton were walking the six blocks from Geismar's dry goods store to their two houses, which were close to each other. This particular Louisiana summer day was sultry, as usual, and as usual they wore shorts. Cassie at eleven was gangly, all arms and legs, with a body that hadn't yet moved into adolescence and a knowledge of the world closer to a child's than to a woman's ("For a smart girl you sure are dumb," her brother often told her). Beth, however, two years her senior, was not only an early bloomer, but a beauty to boot. Her long, shapely legs fit her slender torso just right, or so it seemed to Cassie, and both beautiful parts of her were crowned by thick, blonde curls that rested elegantly on her shoulders.

Seeing Babe in the streets wasn't unusual, but this time he made a clear turn in the girls' direction and began following them, laboring to catch up. When he did, they didn't want to stop as he began muttering something—to Beth, it seemed. They listened more closely as he repeated: "You go' somethin' i' yo' pants I want!" he was saying, gruff and insistent.

"What?" Cassie asked, turning to him.

He repeated a little louder, "You go' somethin' i' yo' pants I want!" as he pointed to Beth's crotch.

The girls didn't hesitate. Like twin deer, they bounded away, down the street toward home, Cassie's long, skinny legs outpacing Beth's racing steps. Within a couple of minutes they had left Babe far behind, waving his arms and muttering in their direction.

When they arrived at Beth's house, they dashed

through the open gate, bolted it behind them, and ran up the steps to the front door, where they paused, heaving and gasping. Cassie, who could wait no longer, turned to Beth, wild-eyed: "Okay, so tell me: What *do* you have in your pants—and how did he know?"

Bigfoot

When the subject of foot binding of little girls in ancient China came up during a conversation with her college girlfriends, Cassie LaPlace couldn't help offering some additional information—more than they wanted to hear, as it happened.

"I read that the tiny female foot in China became an erotic fetish in some circles. One man I read about found it the height of sexual pleasure to put his concubine's tiny, deformed foot all the way into his mouth, in and out, again and again."

"Good heavens! How disgusting!" Kay Goodrich exclaimed. "They took their pleasure from someone else's pain! I'm glad we don't do that kind of thing over here."

"No," Cassie agreed. "We just grow everything as big as we can get it."

"Well, not feet," said Kay. "I'm eighteen and only wear a five-and-a-half."

"What do you know, you little Oriental throwback," Cassie teased her. "Let me tell you what it's like to have Made-in-America feet."

"I was twelve years old," she began, "attending a school-sponsored dance in our gym. The deejay announced that the next dance required each girl to bring a shoe to the center of the dance floor. I wasn't even five feet tall, but I still had huge feet—a size seven-and-a-half—and my black, flat-heeled shoes had extra-long pointed toes. I was a midget wearing gondolas.

"As other girls tossed their shoes into the pile, I added my black boat. Then the boys were sent to pick a shoe and dance with the Cinderella who owned its mate. I'm sure most of the other girls had arranged beforehand for the right boy to find their shoe, but I waited in dread.

"To my horror, my black shoe appeared in the hand of a high school civics teacher, a chaperone for the dance, who was looking around pleasantly for his Cinderella. I wasn't quick enough to hide. When he found me, he seemed as amazed as I was. I put on my shoe, and we shuffled to the dance floor.

"We endured our dance together, moving in tandem without speaking, my arms shooting straight up to reach his shoulder and hand. To this point in my life, it was my most embarrassing three minutes. When I returned to my girlfriends, they were looking at me and giggling, snickering, and snorting. When you're down, there's nothing quite like friendship.

"What made things worse was what my mother, who taught in the same school, told me later the civics teacher had said the day after our dance-floor shuffle—that the thing he had dreaded most about the shoe-dance was the prospect of getting some undersized child for a partner. To avoid that, he had looked for the biggest shoe he could find—mine, as it were. Great. Not only had I been forced into a handlock-of-misery with a high school teacher; I also won the contest for the biggest foot in school.

"But let's go back to that Chinese fetish," Cassie continued. "The fact is that if I ever hook up with someone who wants to put my foot in his mouth, he'd choke to death before he got halfway there, so I guess I don't have to worry about it—and a good thing, too, because my feet are really ticklish."

Favorite Foods

Although Centenary gave Cassie many things, the small, north Louisiana college was the site of her first sustained head-on collision with the non-Cajun world—that is, with what was beyond South Louisiana (she now capitalizes the place, recognizing its status as a country).

The first weeks and months at Centenary were rough. She wrote letters to everyone she'd ever known, telling them how much they'd meant to her and how deeply she treasured them. Her high school English teacher, Dianne Savares, having received one of these, asked her mother if Cassie was all right. It sounded to her, she said, as if she were saying goodbye.

In a way she was. She would never again see St. Aimé as the center of the universe.

There was a Mason-Dixon line of sorts in mid-Louisiana, at about Alexandria, that divided north Louisiana Bible-Belt Protestants from South Louisiana Cajun Catholics, and each group regarded the other with dislike and suspicion. North Louisianians saw Cajuns as immoral—drunkards, gamblers, womanizers, and full-throated sinners of every stripe who behaved wickedly Monday through Saturday but who on Sunday tearfully confessed to everything, recited their Hail Marys, and girded their loins for another week of non-stop sinning. Cajuns, on the other hand, thought of north Louisiana Protestants as shriveled-up, prune-sucking, Bible-thumping life-stranglers who were forever poking around where they had no business, hoping

John LaPlace after squirrel hunting

to get indignant over someone else's good time.

Cassie was a Protestant in South Louisiana, which meant she was both tolerated and tainted. By the time she went to Centenary, she had imprinted some of the Cajun ways—doing the Twist, for example, with a loose-hipped abandon that stopped all action on the dance floor of a Centenary sock hop; she wore too much makeup; and her long blonde hair sported a huge pompadour on top, in the style of the most refined in St. Aimé's inner circle.

So she was hazed with more creative malice than most when she first came to Centenary. She was forced, for example, to walk to class for a week with her hair in thirteen braids, clothes wrong-side-out, pulling a toy dog on rollers behind her. But people there were ultimately more kind than cruel, or maybe they simply got tired; in any case, they began to accept her.

Or so she thought until, one day in the student cafeteria, at a table of seven or eight Centenary girls, the subject of favorite foods came up.

"My favorite by far is fried chicken," Nancy Morcom said, "but I like it best with a little cuplet of honey on the side." Cassie had never heard of honey with chicken but let it pass.

"Give me a thick, juicy steak any day," said Alisha Smith (she came from nearby Texas), "and I like it rare, with lots of A-1, French fries, and green beans cooked in ham hocks!"

And so it went 'round the table. After everyone else had spoken, Carolyn Carpenter turned to Cassie. "And what

Cassie's favorite food

about you? Don't you have a favorite food down there in the bayou?"

"Absolutely!" Cassie said, ready to participate but a little shy. She'd been amazed not to hear her own choice mentioned.

"Squirrel jambalaya," she said, not immediately picking up on the silence that fell or the hands that slowly pulled away from the table. But Cassie figured she needed to elaborate, and so went on:

"Daddy hunts squirrels, you see, and I help clean them—holding their little feet while he cuts the skin off so quickly—it's like pulling off their pyjamas!"

She couldn't tell whether the other girls helped their daddies skin squirrels, since they were looking at her strangely. She went on:

"After we skin them, Mama puts them in a pressure cooker with lots of seasoning, and then she adds rice, until everything is fabulous! It's the best-tasting food in the world. When we were kids we always hoped to get a squirrel head in our serving—"

"You can't be serious!" Nancy Morcom interrupted her, looking disdainful and horrified. "Where did you grow up? In a pirogue? Come on, no one eats squirrels, and I don't think they ever did!"

"Oh, yes, they did—and do!" Cassie said, a bit irritated to be accused of lying. "But hear me out. The best part is next. If we're lucky enough to get a squirrel head, we open their little mouths, then pull out the tongues and eat them. And finally, with our knife blade, we rap the tiny skulls until they crack, and we eat the brains!"

Over the noise of gagging and snorting, Cassie held up her hand: "I know, I know, squirrel brains by themselves aren't the best-tasting thing in the world, but along with everything else, they're the *crème de la crème* of Cajun cuisine—think squirrel ice cream!"

Teenage girls can do disgust more theatrically than any other species. They also have long memories.

II. Eros

Love y'all,
Lynn

Cassie

Cassie Speaks out from Beyond Left Field

Perhaps everyone starts off feeling left out. We succeed by muscling our way into life and, if we're lucky, winning on our terms. Sports is a powerful metaphor because it models how we can win, how we can take a set of circumstances and possibly make it work in our favor. I understand that and in some ways affirm it. But all metaphors and their meanings break down at some point, and when they do, we're sometimes left with no meaning. Do we then continue playing out our lives like some handed-down game? Is winning really the goal? If so, then how important to that victory is the process of getting there? Or, maybe, more accurately, how important to the process is the victory? I offer here some views on the importance of process and the unimportance of victory from someone who sees herself as having lived a metaphor—left out in left field—for most of her early life. I lost every game, caught no important fly, gave no real aid to my team. If the metaphor was about winning, I was a loser—so much so as not to have been in the game at all. But in an elsewhere space outside left field—past metaphor and tangled within the process of struggle—I defined myself and learned that I could love something deeply yet never, ever want to possess it.

It started with being born blond-haired and blue-eyed in a family of brownies—an apparent recessive hiccup, since both grandfathers were blond and blue-eyed, but no one else in either family. I was also the only left-hander, with pigeon toes that required corrective shoes until I was six, making me not only directionally challenged but a stumbler in the wrong direction. One of my earliest memories at about age two occurs in my parents' bed on a Sunday morning, where my four-year-old brother and I would pile in to join my mother and father in drinking café au lait (Carter and I had cups of warm, sweet milk with a couple of tablespoons of dark-roast French coffee), a family-weekend routine. I liked to sit between my mother and father, one hand on Mama's "la-la's" and the other on Daddy's "feathers." I very much wanted "la-la's" when I grew up and definitely didn't want feathers, although I adored those on my father's chest. But the three of them could always make me cry and roll around in misery at the foot of the bed as they sang together, "Beautiful, beautiful brown eyes,/ I'll never love blue eyes again," which they regularly did. That music, in my protesting memory, was my theme song.

Before anyone talked about dyslexia, I was dyslexic. I had trouble processing certain kinds of information, particularly if it involved conceptualizing movement of objects through space. I could never tell left from right, I arranged books in bookcases going in the wrong direction, and I could hardly walk around the block without getting lost. I was told, concerning an IQ test I took at age twelve, that the score was very high overall but that on one part, about abstract spatial perception, I had scored what the counselor, her lips somewhat pursed, called "low normal." I remember that section because it included a series of disembodied hands on a page, some with the hand facing up, others facing down, some the right hand, others the left, at every imaginable angle. We had a short time to mark which hand, right or left, fit each box, and I remember the extraordinary frustration I felt when I completed only about a fourth of that section because I had literally to place my hand in the same position as the hand in the box to have any idea which hand I was seeing. "Let's draw Cassie a picture" was a family chant because I never seemed to get any joke or complex explanation. The only C I ever made in school was in plane geometry, and I felt lucky to get it. I was so clueless that even language, usually my strength, deserted me. One day I asked the geometry teacher what a "circumcised polygon" was. He smiled and said, "One with the top cut off."

I had acne in a culture of perfect complexions, and I was Protestant in a culture of Catholics. I was female in a culture that privileged males, but in an unusual way. Males in South Louisiana were indulged and allowed to remain untamed and immature, while the women, whose model was the Virgin Mary, held everything together, suffered everything, made everything work. In my mother's more Calvinistic language, those views still held, but the women also bore the blame: "If anything goes wrong it's because some woman wasn't doing her job properly," she would say. The women were always responsible. No one could expect anything from the men.

As I grew up, I earned my beyond-left-field position by not finding a place within the stadium of my culture. My mother wanted me to study piano so that I could marry a doctor and play "Smoke Gets in Your Eyes" for ladies' teas. I played that song and loved it, but I loved Bach even more and would have to be asked or sometimes told to stop practicing because I was getting on everyone's nerves. I read not only by the hour but by the week and month and year, in some ways missing out on the kinetic culture around me, for which I substituted the one inside my head. My mother wanted me to be pretty, but I became obsessive about that too. She entered me in my first beauty pageant, but I didn't stop there. "I always wanted a pretty girl," she said, "but I never asked for a peacock!"

No regulating principle. I didn't understand my community, and I couldn't find a place within it where I could thrive. Maybe that's a launching pad for creating something else, or maybe it's a recipe for failure. I do know that I became happier as I grew older and traveled farther and farther away from the place that put the marrow in my bones, the arrow through my heart.

Plaisir d'Amour

Plaisir d'amour ne dure qu'un moment;
chagrin d'amour dure toute la vie.
        —French love song, 1784

The joy of love will dazzle like a flame
the one who circles, seeking its embrace
Love's sorrow sears the heart in endless pain

She searches, restless with desire, to claim
her lover's touch, his scent, his hair, his face—
the joy of love that dazzles like a flame—

then cries and begs him not to leave. In vain
she laughs and tries to snuff out every trace
of love that sears her heart in endless pain

He slips into her dreams to call her name
and, teasing, disappears at her embrace
The joy of love keeps dazzling like a flame

that spreads across her life and seams her brain
with wounds the world and time cannot erase
Love's sorrow sears the heart in endless pain

and the song of love repeats its sweet refrain
as, dizzy, round she goes, caught in the chase:
The joy of love still dazzles like a flame
Its sorrow sears the heart in endless pain

Lynn Hoggard

Love Song for Heraclitus

all things are a flowing

To wake upon the sands of some cold sea
and lie uncountried still beneath a sun
whose hot indifferent rays stir havoc
in my blood and singe my lungs to gasping
for desire; to rise up with the tide
and swim ablaze in airy spirals up—
To soar with fins of flame into the sun!
Let love consume me in candescent lust
Let molten earth swell soulless from my feet
into my eyes, rip from its crust
and shower on the sea my sizzling dust—

I sleep within the depths of some cold sea,
tendered by wandering dreams that sway and sigh
   Take us back to Maya let us die

A Courtly Lady Drops Her Rose

If I were as still
as sta-mened
as the snow lily

and you as certain and
assertive
as the droning bee
plucking nectared notes
upon his
flower—

If we were, then, less alike
than fields of sunning corn—
than the leaping moonstruck waves—
than man and woman—

Lynn Hoggard

Poetry as Lemon

Freud said that art
sublimates
and is
cathartic:
Goethe blew out
Werther's brains,
not his own.

So now
I've written it all down—
externalized, suffused, controlled—
all about the frenzy and the itch—

but when I put my pencil down
my hand
I note
still
trembles.

Mnemonics:
Reciting the Three L's

1.
Loved by my love:
lost in dark woods
of bright flowers

2.
Learned by my love:
taught my own words
in new language

3.
Left by my love:
whisked off the moon
to tumble till Plat-O.

Lynn Hoggard

Leonora in Lafayette, 1884

Mrs. Gautreaux bustles past the window
toward home to end an afternoon of shopping,
and the Millet boys, toting
feed in their hand-pulled, slatted wagon,
and Mrs. Ambeau's maid hurries on some errand—
to buy a ham hock, maybe, for the white beans.

Then a pair of lovers moving toward the sunset
pauses by her window. Her lamp unlighted,
they can't see behind the eyelet curtain.
He plucks a rose that leans beyond the picket fence
and threads his sweetheart's bodice with vermilion stain,
as Leonora falls into a memory:

> *He left the church alone. I followed,*
> *telling Mama of a message for Mrs. Silon—*
> *that I would presently be home.*
> *He stood beside a chinaberry tree*
> *near Templet's road, I behind nandina*
> *till she came.*
> *When they touched, sight blurred.*
> *The doctor said that vapors sent me*
> *to my bed; then weeks of fever came.*

In the low lamplight Leonora
neatly lays aside her clothes, washes
in the porcelain bowl, then, seated at her mirror,

unbinds her brown and graying hair.
Gaze fixed upon herself, she traces
with her hand the length of hair across her breast.
She lifts a flower from the vase
and lies, eyes closed, her heart beneath the rose.
One by one she pulls the petals free, bruising
between her fingers their velvet mold.
Fading, Leonora
slowly rubs the pungent folds again,
again across her lips,
her nose.

Lynn Hoggard

Flying Away on Rio Air

This beast has buzzed into the vortex of my brain
and thrusts propellers whizzing out of either ear
Roaring winds gut every aperture

No choice left:

    jettison
         all
               ballast

Vampire Girl

Tonight I open my window wide;
maybe he won't come.

I lie dreaming I might slip away
but feel again the ache
of a wound being picked open
as he fits his teeth
into the socket on my neck

He's killing me, the no-count
but I don't cry out, don't cry
die
      amoebic—
      ooze   and   pulse—
      wave on wave of sweetness
      rolling through a one-celled universe

      plashing
      sinking
      then leaping up
      a hook through my lip—
      slick and sleek and rainbow-scaled
      I twist and shine in the sun!

I could kill for this!
drop house, car
all my friends

Lynn Hoggard

to crawl on my belly
back into this swamp!

Sated, he rises
over my dead body, withers
into a black leather glove
and flaps off.

I lie dreaming
where I slipped
away.

Torturing the Rat

Hungry
for food
he gnaws
his restless way inside me
bowel to brain
and back

When I feed my rat
filling his belly with bread
with cheese with wine
he falls voluptuously
asleep
inside his temple
outside time

When I fast, my rat
again goes racing
hot to prove the sharpness
of his tooth:
my bleeding knees
my outstretched arms
my wondering look
of love

III. The Storm's Eye

Martha LaPlace was principal at a defining moment

A Defining Moment

Martha LaPlace's finest moment, Cassie later realized, would have had to include a battle. Everything in her mother's nature and in the historic circumstances of St. Aimé during the start of the school year in 1969 had been slowly moving toward confrontation. Now, the sides squared off. One was a group of angry protesters ready to explode unless it could return the community, by force if necessary, to its segregated past. The other was an impromptu, nervous, shifting coalition of educators, churchgoers, and National Guardsmen, who—in different rhythms—all were moving in the same direction.

Fifteen years after the U.S. Supreme Court declared school segregation to be illegal, many Louisiana schools remained in violation of the law, including those in Ascension Parish, where St. Aimé Elementary was located and where Martha LaPlace was principal. With eighteen hundred students, hers was the largest elementary school in the state. Losing patience with the fifteen-year lack of progress in the schools, the federal government mandated integration with the start of the 1969 academic year, and forty black, elementary students were assigned to St. Aimé, with similar situations across the parish. When parish schools tried to open, buses were bombed, two people were killed, and, because of threats or actual violence against school administrators, every school—except for Martha LaPlace's—was closed. For a while the Deep South's double standard—denying women actual power while glorifying their status as madonnas—worked in a woman's favor. But Martha LaPlace happened to be an unusual madonna, with a pioneer's grit and a warrior's resolve, whose roots had pierced the community's bedrock. Starting nearly thirty years before, she had been a teacher at St. Aimé, then a guidance counselor, then the elementary-school principal. She had known most of the picketers since their childhood, when they had been in her classroom—some of them multiple times.

Now those students were men carrying signs, sticks, bats, and perhaps concealed weapons, shuffling about, muttering, and staring menacingly at others. They were angry because the federal government was forcing their hand, but they were also angry because their entitlement as whites was being challenged. They didn't overtly threaten Martha LaPlace, who, after all these years, still intimidated many of them, but on that first day they formed a blockade across the sidewalk of the school's main entrance and refused to let the black children enter.

The next day about two hundred National Guardsmen arrived with rifles, lining either side of the sixty-foot concrete walkway that led from Burnside Street to the school's entrance. The picketers at first formed a tight wad at the far end of the walkway, hoping in that way to keep the children from passing through, but the guardsmen forced the picketers to open a passage. Still, no children dared set foot on the path between the protesters' hovering ranks. That was when Martha LaPlace stepped abruptly forward and took one student by the hand, then another, and began walking toward the entrance. One picketer, a Cajun and her former student, stepped in front of her to block her way, saying almost apologetically, "Aw, Miz LaPlace, I wish you wouldn' do da'."

"Shut up, Cletus Broussard!" she said, eyeing him fixedly. "You were dumb in the second grade, and you're dumb now. Get out of my way!"

"Yez ma'am," he mumbled, stepping aside.

After escorting the first two students, she came back for the next two, then the next, then the next.

Someone in the crowd snarled in her direction, "Nigger-lover!"

Not breaking stride, she turned her head in the speaker's direction and shot back, "White trash!"

Twenty times she made the trip. Finally, with all the children safely inside, the day's classes began.

* * *

She hadn't looked for this particular fight and certainly didn't plan to be its leader. Like most whites in South Louisiana, she resented the government's intervention. "They should have let us work it out," she told her family. "It would have taken longer, but it wouldn't have caused this kind of rage and violence." Like others who shared this view, however, she remained vague about how and when things might have worked themselves out. What pressed her conscience into action was the weight of the law, which she now felt she had personally been handed, and she was fiercely determined to obey it. "I won't become the excuse for my school's continuation to break the law," she told her teachers and administrators, knowing that some in other schools might have used threats of violence as sufficient reason to close their schools.

Day after day she performed this walking ritual and so managed to get the children into the building. But entry into the building was only the beginning of the challenge.

The protesters showed they could be cunning and vicious. A number of the elementary school's buses had their engines blown up, making it harder for children in the densely populated rural areas to get to school. Nails and broken glass were strewn nightly for weeks over the semi-circular driveway that allowed other buses to deposit students inside the school yard. Delivery trucks carrying food to the school cafeteria were met with human barricades of gun-toting men, and the trucks turned back. It looked as though St. Aimé Elementary, having won the first battle, would lose the war.

As if fueled by these obstacles, Martha LaPlace turned to the two groups she could most depend on: her teachers and her Methodist church. The teachers, of course, wanted to teach. Church members, while not necessarily integrationists, believed in Martha LaPlace, who had founded their church, and in John Wesley, whose social gospel required them to help the needy and rescue the distressed. So church members organized groups of men who, every morning in the mists of dawn, swept and cleared the school driveway of the nails, glass, bricks, and tree limbs that littered it, and the women of the church, with the help of dozens of parents and teachers, organized, prepared, and delivered hundreds of sandwiches—daily—to feed the children and keep the doors of the school open.

When it began to look as though the school would remain open, the protesters got personal. They burned crosses on Martha and John LaPlace's lawn, slashed tires and broke windows of their cars, and threatened to burn their house. Cassie, at home for a few days, was about to return to college. Although she didn't know it until twenty years later, her mother had received a telephone call about her: "We know you got a daughter alone in that house," the voice had said: "She gonna get raped—real bad." A man from her mother's church, a blacksmith, sat in their living room or paced his way through their house all day while Cassie was there, a shotgun in his hands. "They say they're gonna burn the house," he told her by way of explanation, nodding toward the outside. "We're not gonna let 'em."

Martha LaPlace knew better than to take her husband's stand on these issues for granted, but she couldn't continue to defy the protesters if he disagreed. If he had said he opposed her resistance, she might have backed down. Their home was his as well as hers. Even less pro-integration than Martha, John LaPlace was essentially a gentle man who had grown up on the South Louisiana levee, where racial preju- dice ran deep and raw. He had been forced to confront his limitations a few years before when Martha had invited her black assistant principal, Darren Roberts, to the house one afternoon after school to try out the family's new pool table,

Protesters threatened to burn their home

which John LaPlace had bought from a local bar and put in his garage. When he walked into the house from work, John was surprised to see the man shooting pool in his garage, but he nevertheless greeted Mr. Roberts politely. Then he disappeared. Martha found her husband sitting on a small stool in their bathroom—the place farthest from the garage— his head in his hands. "Honey, I know I'm wrong," he said, shaking his head from side to side, "but I just can't go out there yet. I just can't."

The home they'd spent twenty years dreaming and building might go up in flames. They and their children could be assaulted, wounded, even killed. Sitting at the kitchen table late one night, they talked about these things. John asked his wife how she felt about the risks. She answered, "If we back down, they win. I don't want them to win."

"So what do you want me to do?" he asked.

"I want us to stand together. I want us to make them lose!" she said. "If they burn the house, we can build another. I don't think they'll hurt you or the younger children. Cassie's being protected. If they kill me, I can stand justified before my god. But if they win—" she paused, losing her words. "We might save our house, but we wouldn't save our dignity. We'd have cratered. I'd rather die! It's finally come down to one thing: In this fight, the community is you and me."

He paused, looking down at his hands as if they held playing cards he needed to consult. If he saw something there, he remained the consummate poker player. He simply looked up at Martha and said, "I'm in."

* * *

The story, of course, doesn't end here. Random violence continued for months, tires were slashed again and then again, threats were made, friendships broken. But St. Aimé Elementary School stayed open. Before many months had passed, the school's struggles returned where they needed to be, to the learning inside the classrooms rather than the violence outside.

Martha LaPlace continued to play her role as prime-mover in her community, but her example remained most powerful among the teachers and students in her school. One day one of those students, Gloria Guidry, who had held Martha LaPlace's hand as they walked through the picket lines, came to her in the school hallway, slipped her hand into Martha's, and said, "Thanks, Miz LaPlace, for all you done to help us."

Martha LaPlace turned to face the child. Taking Gloria's hand in both her own and squeezing it, she leaned toward the student and said, "Thank you, Gloria, for telling me that. Now, Sweetheart, let's have you tell me that one more time, and this time say, 'Thanks for all you *did*'."

Lynn Hoggard

The Road Ahead

Dead
in the road ahead—
black cat

Small thing, this end to life—
a sharp panic, a thud,
a bump,
a spreading pool of red,
and, finally, a smear—

run over
run over
run over
run over

Burning Man

"Bummer!" Cassie LaPlace said out loud, though no one was in earshot. She was trudging toward the school bus, toting her piccolo, and feeling hot in her green and gold band uniform, in spite of the sharp, damp cold of the South Louisiana winter. Not only had St. Aimé lost its Friday-night football game to Thibodeaux, but a long bus ride home awaited her. As usual on game days she'd been too excited to eat, and now her stomach was growling. Along with the ninety-nine other members of the St. Aimé High School Marching 100, she'd played her heart out during the game on feisty march tunes like "Washington Post," relishing the extra piccolo trills and arabesques that Mr. Delano, their director, had written for her; and she, like the others, had done her best on the half-time show they'd worked on all week, staying after school three hours most afternoons to get the music and field formations right. Most of those who attended the games used half time to get snacks or visit friends. Only a few paid attention, and, of those, only rarely would one tell band members they had done a good job. Not knowing anything else, the musicians hardly cared. Like Cassie, young and filled with her own energy, they rode high on the current, carried by its momentum. That was enough. Now it was over, and she felt tired and hungry. "Empty," she said aloud, a little more softly, as she grabbed the step-railing and climbed into the bus.

"There'll be no singing tonight!" she thought as she located her place on the front row of seats—the monitor's seat—just behind the driver. As a senior and a band officer, she was in charge of making sure everyone got on board and more or less behaved during the trip home. When St. Aimé won, exhilaration swept exhaustion aside, and band members sang raucously, sometimes the whole trip home, including their version of the "Notre Dame Fight Song"— "Beer, beer for St. Aimé High"—or run up and down the aisles until the bus driver or Cassie made them stop.

But this night, they'd lost. Her friends Joycelyn, Rosemary, and Annette sat behind her, but she didn't feel like talking, and they didn't seem interested either, each fallen into her own thoughts. Everyone brooded as the bus chuffed its way home, benches rocking and creaking with the rhythms of the road and the weight of their bodies. "Maybe," Cassie thought, trying to conjure enthusiasm, "I'll order a chili dog at Tucker's," the snack bar across the street from the school, where they would be deposited in a couple of hours. She settled in, hoping the trip would pass quickly.

Sitting just behind the driver, Mr. Babin, Cassie saw ahead of her that portion of the almost-deserted four-lane highway that he saw. As the bus sped through the darkness, something furtive caught her eye. At first she had no idea what it was—some kind of flickering, zig-zagging spark in the distance, like a firefly, but she knew a firefly wouldn't be visible that far away. She felt a sudden chill—no, more like a small flame—race just beneath the surface of her skin, and she noticed the driver straighten in his seat, giving full attention to what lay ahead. The bus slowed, rolling closer.

The zig-zagging flicker suddenly shot across the

highway at a right angle, then came abruptly to a halt. From about thirty yards away Cassie could see that the flicker had turned into a rolling ball of flames. Now about thirty feet away, the bus pulled to a stop. That was when the ball of flames unfolded—into arms, legs, a torso and head—standing immobile for an instant before it began racing back and forth across the highway, arms spiraling.

The driver pulled the bus to the side of the highway. When he yanked the lever that opened the bus doors, Cassie heard for the first time the screams of the burning man—sounds of an agony so piercing that it obliterated everything else. In paralyzed horror, she watched the man, still screaming, fall, try to get up, then fall again, rolling crazily in all directions. The driver ripped off his bomber jacket as he raced to the man and began slapping the flames, rolling the man back and forth again and again. After a while, the burning stopped, along with the man's screams.

Everyone in the bus was screaming, shouting, or sobbing. Cassie, who had gone as far as to step outside the bus onto the grass, didn't scream, but neither did she move to help the man or go back to the bus to help those inside, still in a panic. Trapped in her own cataclysm, she stood transfixed, taken over by an uncontrollable trembling, unable to speak, move, or even know that she could do none of these things. Engulfed in the image of the burning man, she could only bear witness to something beyond any imagining she had ever known. When she collapsed she still didn't cry. She curled into a ball that rocked back and forth on the grass.

The police arrived, then the ambulances. Band members, including Cassie and a few others who had stumbled outside the bus, were put back inside and instructed to sit tight until all the necessary information could be gathered. In an hour or so, the bus was sent on its way. Once home, Cassie went straight to bed, where she lay not sleeping that night and many nights to come. She learned a few days later that the man—a boy of sixteen—had been riding his motor-cycle on the highway when the gasoline tank exploded. He didn't survive the explosion. But in another way he lived on—inside Cassie—where he's still burning.

"Your world a baseball diamond"

The Game Daddy Won

Your hardened athlete's heart exploded
at 4:10 a.m.; you heaved
and pitched across the room
the Alka-Seltzer Mother handed you,
fell shouting on the pillows.
Fists clenched across your chest,
you prayed a final inning's end.

Daddy, they've struck you out,
cancelled your career, torn to bits
the contract you'd always dreamed:

> *Your world a baseball diamond*
> *shaped something like a human heart,*
> *whose veins were chalked in blood*
> *where all, all pumped in pressured joy*
> *to hard rhythms that you, centrally mounded, made.*

Now you lounge down low, where teams
of boozy veins eternally unwind.
Expansively off-season, you'll sink oblivious
to mounds of satin dust.

What fan is left to tell your other story—
the grandstand play you didn't mean to make—
the way you pitched a shut-out to my mother
who, crying, cheered your dug-out heart's low throbs

Lynn Hoggard

and swelled your children, blinking scoreboards,
with her own heart's sobs?

A Diminished Triad

holds three tones together
in brooding harmony—
Paris, Christmas, me—

a mustard-walled hotel room
an aching suitcase
the bells of Sacré Coeur, wild with loss

Lynn Hoggard

Reunion

When the sun falls down
through haze

his vague hands
part the clouds

My father leans
a star-point gaze
of patience

I miss him
then
I miss him

Antistrophe

You held out your arms
as I came to your bed
You smiled, touching
my hair, my face
You whispered my name
and kissed my hands

You would have gone with him
but they pulled you back
cutting the band
from your swollen finger
It lay in your lap
a broken maidenhead
an exit from wife to widow

We cried. Our fingers
like frightened survivors
sought the warmth
of each other's touch

> On the day I knew
> the fullness of your love
> without your hate
> my father, like the sword
> between us, fell
> and I came halfway over the earth
> to hold you, my mother

Lynn Hoggard

I came
your daughter

Elektra

In My Dream

my mother is giving me
her almost-new Cadillac
that she spent so much on
since the flood
having the snakes removed

but because she's been bitten
so many times
she's giving it up
and hands the keys
to me.

Lynn Hoggard

Dementia

Grieving, she bows over herself
and weaves mauve tulle into knots
tulle into knots
tulle into knots

They're strewn across her room
like clots she can't think through
She tears, wads, rips them
trying to remember how
to thread the tulle another way

> into bows, then wreaths
> that hang on doors
> that circle life around her meaning
> that show others her Thanksgiving

Let's see, she mutters, tries again—
This end of tulle goes—where?
> *I have to make my bows—*
> *I have to make my bows!*
> *They have to go in flower bunches*
> *we call them—what?*
Bouquets, I whisper.

She weaves another knot of tulle
another clot of tulle—blot of rule—plot of fool!

Let's see, how does a poem end?
    Not this way, please—
    Don't let it end like this—

        My mother weaves her death wreath
            knot of tulle
            by knot of tulle
            by knot

Lynn Hoggard

Affirmation

is something she'll never give you,
my friend said:
So learn that.

She's given what she can
and is dying.

So learn this:
Give her what
she didn't give to you.

Affirm her life
and show your love.

It's up to you
to make the circle
whole.

It's True, Whether It Happened or Not

Before she died, she told me,

I was proud and strong,
a lonely fighter
who wouldn't put her weapons down
even when the enemy was gone,

so I was hard, so hard
on you, your brothers,
and your sister,
but I hope you know

I loved you the way oceans
love the moon: you shaped
my heaving breaths.
I fought those wars
with shadows of myself.

Lynn Hoggard

Gift to the Goddess

Arabesques of lapis and cornelian
surround a small ivory carving
from Nimrud, ninth century BCE:
a lioness and man in a gold-leaf bower.

A jewel on her brow, her breast
against his supine breast, the lioness rules.
As she cradles him with a paw
her bite in his neck goes deep.

His face, serenely raised,
ebbs into ecstasy.
Hers, serenely bowed, receives
all of him.

Lioness and Man

Kaleidoscope in White

White is at the intersection of blue and green and yellow
and red.... The thrust must go through to the white.
—William Carlos Williams

Colors come to life before my eyes
to sing a soul in rhythm-colored tune:
kaleidoscopic dancing in the skies!

A yellow sun draws others where it lies
to splash them spinning wide again, and soon
these colors come to life before my eyes

A bud of green discarding its disguise
unfolds into a parasol of bloom—
kaleidoscopic dancing in the skies—

When rubied heart bursts open and defies
the deeper tones that tilt into the gloom
then colors come to life before my eyes

and call and call my song. Though body dies
some swirling, blue-flecked winter afternoon
(kaleidoscopic dancing of the skies)

An arc of sun-streaked rainbow lifts and guides
the sod of sighs away, up to the moon—

Lynn Hoggard

and white song leaps to life before my eyes—
kaleidoscopic—dancing through the skies!

Guarding the Mystery

...the fire, the fire inside!
    —John of the Cross

Deep in the soul
is a cave where someone kneels
mouthing sounds I cannot understand
She speaks to a fire
mirrored in her eyes
I know that what she does is the center
of everything important.

  The way began simply
  with insomnia—the brain gone night-clubbing again
  the body cross and sharp-tongued
  at being dragged from one image to another
  When the pair finally collapses across
  some table, arms entwined, the soft tap-
  tapping of the tiny mallet at the skull
  starts again, the world demanding
  to be let back in

  It enters as a burning wood
  guarded by a lion
  Small, frightened things run from fire
  and are torn apart, entrails devoured first
  the creature an ecstasy
  of destruction and desire
  the way not quiet or kind

Lynn Hoggard

Even now, searching as I run
it runs, eyes foraging

I fast. In a little corner
with a little book, to live content
with just enough!
But the walls will not stay tight
Sounds enter and water seeps, forcing me
to listen and live on tiptoe
The walls float apart
on rushing waves
as swift, deep currents
carry me away
I reach to all the ones I love
who rush past me
blowing kisses, waving goodbye
Nothing I do can save them
Nothing can save me
from the terror of their beauty

Now in the cave
someone stands before a fire
and holds a knife
With a moan, she carves
her chest and lifts her heart
to the flames
singing as it burns
swaying as the fire sways
laughing as it snaps

Mouthing sounds I cannot understand
she turns to me
I see the burning in her eyes
I see the flame behind her
I see—I see!

Her eyes—her eyes the fire!

www.ingramcontent.com/pod-product-compliance
Lightning Source LLC
Chambersburg PA
CBHW072146090426
42739CB00013B/3293